CHRIS BERRYWORTH

Funds for Festivities

How to Save Money on Holiday Gifts and Presents

Contents

Introduction

In the hustle and bustle of everyday life, the holiday season often sneaks up on us faster than we anticipate. The joy of giving gifts to our loved ones can quickly turn into stress when we're faced with the reality of our bank accounts. This is where a well-structured gift savings plan comes to the rescue, allowing us to navigate the holiday season with financial confidence and the ability to create meaningful memories without breaking the bank.

It's essential to approach holiday gift-giving with a thoughtful and financially responsible mindset. Budgeting for holiday gifts isn't just about numbers on a spreadsheet; it's a deliberate strategy that empowers you to navigate the festive season with financial confidence, joy, and a genuine spirit of giving.

The Importance of Budgeting for Holiday Gifts

Budgeting for holiday gifts is a proactive approach that transforms the act of gift-giving from a potential financial burden into a thoughtful and well-planned gesture. It empowers you to:

1. Maintain Financial Stability

A well-structured gift budget ensures that your holiday celebrations don't compromise your financial stability. By allocating a specific amount to gifts, you're setting boundaries that prevent overspending and safeguard your overall financial health.

2. Reduce Stress and Anxiety

Financial stress can cast a pall over even the most joyous occasions. Budgeting for gifts eliminates the stress of wondering how you'll manage the expenses, allowing you to fully immerse yourself in the holiday festivities.

3. Make Thoughtful Choices

Budgeting encourages thoughtful and deliberate gift choices. Rather than hastily purchasing items without considering their value or utility, you'll have the time and space to find gifts that truly resonate with the recipients.

4. Avoid Post-Holiday Regrets

We've all experienced the "buyer's remorse" that comes with overspending during the holidays. Budgeting prevents post-holiday regrets by ensuring that your spending aligns with your financial capacity.

5. Embrace the True Spirit of Giving

The heart of gift-giving lies in the sentiment behind the presents, not their monetary value. A budgeted approach allows you to focus on the thought and love behind each gift, enhancing the emotional impact of your gesture.

6. Plan for Future Goals

Budgeting for gifts doesn't exist in isolation; it's a component of responsible financial planning. By managing your gift expenses, you're freeing up resources that can be directed toward savings, investments, or other financial goals.

A Holistic Approach to Gift Budgeting

Creating a gift savings plan isn't about restricting your generosity; it's about lining up your gift-giving aspirations with your financial reality. It's an opportunity to prioritize both your relationships and your financial well-being. Throughout this comprehensive guide, we'll explore a range of strategies and techniques that empower you to navigate the holiday season with confidence and grace.

From crafting a personalized gift savings plan to exploring creative DIY gift ideas, from utilizing technology to find the best deals to leveraging your skills for extra income, this guide is a road map to holistic gift budgeting. As we journey through the chapters, you'll discover how to strike a balance between heartfelt giving and responsible financial stewardship.

Remember, a well-thought-out gift savings plan isn't just a financial tool; it's a gesture of self-care and mindfulness. By embracing this approach, you're nurturing your own well-being while expressing your love and appreciation for those who matter most. So, let's embark on this journey together, and by the time the next holiday season arrives, you'll be equipped with the knowledge and tools to celebrate with joy, intention, and financial peace.

The Gift Savings Plan

The Gift Savings Plan

The Gift Savings Plan is your compass, guiding you through the process of setting achievable goals, breaking down your holiday expenses, and establishing a realistic timeline for savings. By the time you finish reading this chapter, you'll be armed with a comprehensive plan that ensures your financial well-being and allows you to give meaningful gifts to your loved ones.

Setting Annual Gifting Goals

The first step in creating a gift savings plan is to set clear and realistic gifting goals for the year. Start by making a list of the people you intend to give gifts to throughout the season, including birthdays, holidays, anniversaries, and other special occasions taking place during this time of the year. Next to each name, jot down a rough idea of the type of gift you'd like to give and the approximate amount you're willing to spend.

For instance, if your sister's birthday is in November and

you'd like to buy her a special piece of jewelry, estimate the cost based on your budget. Similarly, if you're planning to host a Christmas dinner and exchange gifts with your extended family, calculate an approximate total for all the gifts combined.

Remember, the key here is to be realistic. While it's wonderful to want to give generously, it's equally important to ensure that your goals align with your financial capacity. This prevents overspending and allows you to stick to your budget.

Breaking Down the Budget

Once you have an estimate of the total amount you'll need for gifts, it's time to break down the budget into manageable segments. Divide the total amount by the number of months remaining until your first gift-giving occasion. This will give you a monthly savings target.

Let's say you estimate that you'll need $1,200 for all your gift-giving occasions this year, and there are eight months left until your first gift-giving occasion (let's assume it's Christmas). Your monthly savings target would be $150 ($1,200 ÷ 8). This approach helps you avoid last-minute financial stress by spreading out the savings over several months.

In essence, breaking down the budget transforms the seemingly daunting task of saving for gifts into a manageable and sustainable process. It empowers you to take control of your finances, plan ahead effectively, and enjoy the holiday season without the burden of financial strain. By allocating a specific amount of money each month, you create a sense of financial security that allows you to focus on the joy of giving rather than worrying about how to afford it.

Creating a Realistic Plan

As you establish your Gift Savings Plan, remember that realism is key. While it's tempting to allocate significant funds for gifts, it's important to ensure that your plan matches your overall financial goals. Your holiday generosity should not compromise your ability to meet essential expenses, pay bills, or work towards long-term objectives.

Consider your current financial situation, including your income, debts, and savings goals. Evaluate the amount you can comfortably set aside for gifts without straining your finances. Remember, the joy of gift-giving doesn't solely depend on the monetary value of the present – thoughtfulness and consideration often hold more significance.

Staying Flexible and Adaptable

Life is full of surprises, and your gift savings plan should be adaptable enough to accommodate unexpected changes. While meticulous planning and budgeting are essential, unforeseen circumstances can arise at any moment, potentially impacting your budgeting efforts. It's important to acknowledge that life is dynamic, and unexpected expenses or changes in financial circumstances can occur.

If you receive a bonus at work or find ways to cut expenses in other areas, consider allocating a portion of these windfalls to your gift savings fund. On the flip side, if unforeseen expenses arise, be prepared to adjust your monthly savings target accordingly. It's a good idea to establish a cushion within your budget to accommodate such fluctuations. Having an emergency fund or a small buffer specifically dedicated to holiday-related surprises can prevent undue stress and financial strain.

Being flexible also extends to your gifting goals. If you find that your initial estimates were too ambitious or not sufficient, don't hesitate to adjust your budget. The goal is to create a plan that serves your financial well-being and allows you to give from a place of genuine care and generosity.

Spreading Savings Over Multiple Months

The concept of spreading savings over multiple months is a cornerstone of effective financial planning. When it comes to budgeting for holiday gifts, this practice takes on even greater significance, offering a blueprint for financial success that ensures you can provide thoughtful gifts without straining your budget or resorting to last-minute panic.

Shifting from Financial Strain to Comfort

The holiday season often comes with a surge in expenses, from gifts and decorations to festive gatherings. The beauty of spreading savings over multiple months lies in its ability to alleviate financial strain. Instead of confronting a hefty bill in a single month, you're proactively setting aside funds over an extended period. This shift from reactive spending to proactive saving transforms your financial outlook, replacing stress with a sense of control and preparedness.

By budgeting a consistent amount each month for your holiday gifts, you avoid the need to dip into emergency funds or rely on credit cards. This financial fortitude not only benefits your holiday budget but also contributes to your overall financial well-being.

Building a Cushion for Unexpected Expenses

Life is unpredictable, and unexpected expenses can easily disrupt even the most meticulously crafted budget. While creating a well-thought-out budget is essential, being flexible and adaptable to unforeseen circumstances is equally crucial. An emergency fund acts as a financial safety net that can cushion the impact of unexpected expenses. This fund should ideally cover three to six months' worth of essentials, including housing, utilities, groceries, and loan payments.

Devote a portion of your budget to a "miscellaneous" or "unforeseen expenses" category. This can serve as a buffer for any unexpected costs that may arise. Whether it's a medical bill, car repair, or unforeseen household repair, you're equipped to handle such emergencies without compromising your gift-giving plans. If a sudden expense emerges, perhaps you temporarily dial back on entertainment expenses to refill your emergency fund, or opt for homemade meals instead of dining out to cover the unanticipated cost. You might trim your monthly subscriptions or delay a vacation, channeling those resources toward addressing the unexpected instead.

Enhancing Flexibility and Adaptability

Budgeting for gifts in a concentrated time frame can lead to rigidity and stress, especially if unexpected financial needs arise. Spreading savings over multiple months enhances your financial flexibility. If a particular month poses additional financial challenges, you have the flexibility to adjust your gift savings slightly without jeopardizing your overall plan.

For instance, if you encounter higher-than-expected utility bills during a hot summer month, you can slightly reduce that month's gift savings contribution while maintaining your overall target. This adaptability ensures that your gift savings plan remains sustainable and responsive to your evolving financial landscape.

If an unexpected expense arises, resist the urge to abandon your budget altogether. Instead, adapt your budget by reallocating funds from non-essential categories to cover the unforeseen cost. This pivot will not only build a habit of staying on track financially in the short term, but also shifting your resources as necessary for larger goals in the long term.

Cultivating a Sense of Achievement

Setting a goal to save a specific amount each month for your gift fund empowers you with a tangible objective to work toward. As each month passes and you consistently contribute to your fund, a sense of achievement builds. You're not only safeguarding your holiday budget but also nurturing your financial discipline and responsibility.

The journey of spreading savings over multiple months

is a testament to your commitment to responsible financial stewardship. Celebrate each successful month as a milestone on the path to accomplishing your gift-giving goals. This sense of accomplishment extends beyond your holiday preparations, positively influencing your overall financial mindset.

Embracing a Season of Joyful Giving

Spreading savings over multiple months is a transformative approach to holiday gift planning. It empowers you to give meaningful presents without compromising your financial stability or resorting to hasty decisions. By embracing this practice, you're embracing the essence of joyful giving – the ability to offer thoughtful and heartfelt gifts while maintaining a balanced and resilient financial foundation.

Remember that spreading savings over multiple months isn't limited to holiday gifts; it's a mindset that can guide your financial decisions year-round. No matter the occasion for the gift, it's empowering to be able to give it from a place of joy. With each month's contribution, you're not just saving for gifts – you're saving for peace of mind, security, and the freedom to enjoy the holiday season without financial worries.

Wrapping It All Up

Creating a gift savings plan is a practical and empowering strategy that allows you to give meaningful gifts without sacrificing your financial stability. By setting annual gifting goals, breaking down your budget, utilizing specialized tools, automating savings, and staying flexible, you'll be well-equipped to navigate the holiday season with confidence and joy. A well-executed gift savings plan ensures that you can express your feelings through thoughtful gestures while maintaining a healthy financial outlook. So, embark on this journey of financial mindfulness, and experience the true magic of giving within your means.

The gift savings plan serves as your strategic ally in the world of holiday budgeting. It breaks down your gift expenses into manageable portions, sets achievable monthly savings targets, and provides a road map for a stress-free holiday season. By spreading savings over multiple months and creating a realistic plan, you're setting yourself up for success. The effort you invest in crafting this plan will undoubtedly yield the joy of giving meaningful gifts without financial strain. As you move forward, keep your eyes on your goals, adjust the plan as needed, and embrace the journey towards a joyful holiday experience.

Cash Envelope System

In the realm of personal finance, the cash envelope system stands as a tried-and-true method that has helped several individuals regain control over their spending, prioritize their financial goals, and cultivate disciplined money management habits. This system, which operates on the principle of using physical envelopes to distribute specific amounts of cash for various spending categories, has gained popularity for its simplicity, effectiveness, and ability to promote mindful spending. In this chapter, you will learn the ins and outs of the cash envelope system and how it can be used in your holiday budget.

Understanding the Cash Envelope System

The cash envelope system offers a tangible and effective way to regain control of your spending and savings. At its essence, it is a budgeting technique that relies on physical cash to manage your expenses. It operates on the principle that once you allocate a specific amount of cash to a certain category, you can't spend more in that category until the next budgeting period.

This method is particularly powerful for curbing impulsive spending and encouraging mindful financial decisions.

How It Works

1. Category Allocation: Start by identifying various spending categories such as groceries, entertainment, dining out, and, in the context of this chapter, gifts and holiday expenses.

2. Cash Distribution: Determine how much you're willing to spend in each category for a given period, such as a week or a month. For instance, if your holiday gift budget is $300, set aside $300 in cash to be placed in the designated envelope.

3. Envelope Labeling: Create physical envelopes for each spending category. Label them clearly, and place the predetermined amount of cash inside each envelope. This serves as a visual reminder of your budget limit.

4. Spending Constraint: When you're ready to make a purchase within a specific category, withdraw the necessary cash from the corresponding envelope. Once the cash in an envelope is depleted, spending in that category stops until the next budgeting period.

5. Tracking and Adjustment: Regularly assess your spending, and if necessary, adjust the cash allocation for each category based on your evolving needs and priorities.

Embracing the Practical Benefits

The cash envelope system offers unique benefits that distinguish it from digital budgeting methods.

Heightened Awareness and Mindful Spending

Unlike swiping a card or clicking "Checkout" online, using physical cash creates a tangible connection to your spending. Counting out cash and seeing it physically leave your hand can make you more conscious of your financial choices.

Natural Spending Limits

Cash envelopes inherently impose spending limits. When the envelope is empty, you can't overspend in that category, promoting thoughtful consideration of each purchase. Once the cash is depleted, you'll need to wait until the next budgeting period before making additional purchases in that category.

Reduced Impulse Spending

The tangible nature of physical cash fosters a direct connection to your spending. The act of physically removing money from an envelope can deter impulsive purchases. Instead of succumbing to impulse buying or unchecked spending, you're compelled to consider if a purchase aligns with your priorities and budgetary allocations.

Avoidance of Debt

Since you're spending only the money you physically have, there's no risk of accumulating credit card debt. By adhering to the limits set by your cash envelopes, you'll steer clear of post-holiday debt that often results from unchecked credit card usage.

Simplified Tracking

With separate envelopes for each spending category, tracking your expenses becomes straightforward. You don't need to log into apps or review statements. The transparency of the envelope system makes it easy to see where your money is going.

Enhanced Accountability

The envelopes themselves act as a built-in accountability system. You can instantly see if you've overspent in a category, prompting you to reassess and adjust accordingly. This sense of accountability encourages you to stick to your budget and make choices that are in alignment with your financial goals, even when tempted by impulse buys.

Flexibility and Customization

The cash envelope system is highly adaptable. You can create envelopes for different purposes, whether it's holiday gifts, groceries, or entertainment. This flexibility ensures that you're in control of your entire financial landscape.

Allocating Funds for Gifts and Holiday Expenses

Allocating funds for gifts and holiday expenses is a pivotal aspect of the cash envelope system, enabling you to navigate the festive season without financial stress. Create dedicated envelopes tailored to your seasonal needs.

Gifts Envelope

Designate an envelope specifically for holiday gifts. Determine the total amount you're willing to spend on gifts during the holiday season and place that amount in the envelope.

Decorations and Parties Envelope

If you're planning to host gatherings or decorate your home for the holidays, create an envelope for these expenses. Include funds for decorations, party supplies, and any hosting-related costs.

Travel and Accommodation Envelope

If you're traveling during the holidays, budget cash for transportation, lodging, and any related expenses.

Miscellaneous Envelope

Anticipate unexpected holiday costs by setting up an envelope for miscellaneous expenses that might arise.

Staying on Course

Staying on course is often the key to turning financial aspirations into tangible realities. The envelope system, with its physical and tangible nature, offers a unique and powerful way to enhance your financial discipline and hold yourself accountable throughout your journey. Whether you're aiming to save money for holiday gifts or any other financial goal, mastering the art of staying focused and accountable within the envelope system can yield remarkable results.

Regularly Monitor Spending

Keep a close eye on your spending in each category. Set aside time each week to evaluate your spending in each category. This practice not only helps you stay on track but also offers an opportunity to adjust your allocations if necessary. If you find that you consistently overspend in a particular area, it might be an indication that you need to adjust your envelope limit or reevaluate your priorities.

Prioritize Needs Over Wants

As you make purchases, prioritize essential items and experiences over frivolous wants. It's natural to encounter tempting opportunities to spend outside your designated envelopes, especially during holiday sales or when faced with enticing deals. When confronted with such situations, pause and consider the long-term impact on your overall budget.

Rollover or Reallocate

If you find that you've under-spent in one category, you have the flexibility to either roll over the excess funds to the next budgeting period or reallocate them to a different envelope. If you find that certain envelopes consistently run out of funds before the end of the month, analyze the underlying reasons and adjust your budget accordingly.

Adjust as Needed

As the holiday season progresses, you might need to adjust your allocations based on unforeseen circumstances. Unexpected expenses or changes in plans can arise, and having the ability to adjust your envelope allocations accordingly can prevent frustration and derailment. If you need to move funds from one envelope to another due to unforeseen circumstances, do so without hesitation. The goal is to maintain your overall budgeting strategy while accommodating necessary shifts.

Seek Support and Accountability

Enlist the support of a friend, family member, or accountability partner who can provide encouragement and hold you responsible for adhering to your cash envelope system. Sharing your goals with someone who understands your financial aspirations can help you stay motivated and committed. Regular discussions about envelope balances, spending decisions, and adjustments your progress and challenges with your support system can also offer fresh perspectives and potential solutions.

Celebrate Financial Freedom

Acknowledging your achievements, no matter how small, is crucial to maintaining motivation. Celebrate milestones such as successfully sticking to your cash envelope budget for a specific period or avoiding unnecessary expenses. These celebrations don't need to be extravagant – they can be as simple as treating yourself to a small indulgence or engaging in a cost-free activity that brings joy.

Harnessing the Envelope Method's Potential

The envelope method's power lies in its ability to transform abstract financial intentions into concrete actions. By staying focused and accountable within this system, you're maximizing its potential to guide you toward your goals. Whether it's saving money for holiday gifts, paying off debt, or building an emergency fund, the envelope method serves as a reliable compass that keeps you on course. As you continue to use this method and experience its impact, you'll realize that staying focused and accountable isn't just a financial strategy – it's a mindset that empowers you to take control of your financial destiny.

By incorporating physical cash into your budgeting approach, you harness these benefits to create a more conscientious and purposeful relationship with your finances. The tactile experience of handling cash heightens your awareness, encourages moderation, and empowers you to make financial decisions that reflect your values and aspirations. Staying disciplined and accountable with the cash envelope method requires dedication and an ongoing commitment to your financial goals. By implementing these strategies and adapting them to your unique circumstances, you'll navigate challenges with resilience and experience the long-term benefits of this budgeting approach.

Wrapping It All Up

To successfully integrate the cash envelope system into your life, start by setting clear budget limits for each category. Assign funds to envelopes at the beginning of your budgeting period, whether it's weekly or monthly. As you make purchases, consistently use the corresponding envelopes, and periodically evaluate your spending habits to identify areas for improvement. This method isn't just about managing money; it's about reshaping your financial mindset and fostering intentional financial habits that can be used throughout the whole year.

Opening a Savings Account

Benefits of a Savings Account

Opening a savings account comes with a host of benefits that can significantly enhance your financial planning and holiday experiences. This specialized account is not just a simple repository for funds; it's a strategic tool that empowers you to approach the holiday season with confidence and peace of mind. This chapter will explore the different types of accounts that are available and strategies to make the most out of them for your holiday budget.

Dedicated Purpose

Your savings account serves as a dedicated vessel for your holiday funds. By creating a distinct space for your gift-related finances, you're safeguarding these funds from being unintentionally spent on other expenses throughout the year and will have them ready for your gift-giving endeavors. This clear separation ensures that when the holiday season arrives, you have a pool of funds.

Financial Organization

Keeping your holiday funds in a separate account brings a new level of financial organization to your plan. You can easily track the growth of your savings over time, set milestones, and measure your progress toward your gift budget goals. This level of transparency makes it simpler to adjust your savings strategy if necessary, ensuring that you remain on target.

Reduced Stress

One of the most significant benefits of a Christmas savings account is the reduction of financial stress during the holiday season. Many people find themselves burdened by mounting credit card bills after the holidays, which can take months to repay. With a special savings account, you're essentially prepaying for your holiday expenses, eliminating the need to rely on credit cards or dip into your regular savings.

Avoiding Last-Minute Panic

The holidays often bring a flurry of expenses, from gifts to travel and festive activities. By opening a savings account, you're effectively distributing the financial burden across the year. This prevents last-minute panic as the holiday season approaches, as you'll already have the necessary funds set aside to cover your anticipated expenses.

Interest Accumulation

Many financial institutions offer interest-bearing savings accounts, meaning that your funds will grow over time. While the interest may not be substantial, it's an additional incentive that rewards your commitment to saving. Over the months leading up to the holidays, even a modest interest accumulation can contribute positively to your gift budget.

Mindful Spending

Having a designated account for holiday savings encourages more mindful spending. Knowing that you have a finite pool of funds allocated for gifts and celebrations prompts you to make thoughtful purchasing decisions. Having this awareness can lead to prioritizing meaningful gifts and experiences over impulsive buys or excessive spending.

Flexibility and Planning

A holiday savings account provides the flexibility to plan well in advance. As the year progresses, you can adjust your savings strategy based on changing circumstances, unexpected expenses, or evolving gift ideas. This flexibility allows you to maintain control over your financial journey while still enjoying the festive spirit of the holiday season.

Available options for Savings Accounts

Christmas Club Accounts

One popular option is the Christmas club account, offered by many credit unions and smaller banks. With this account, you regularly deposit funds throughout the year, and the bank "releases" the accumulated funds to you in November, perfectly timed for holiday shopping. Christmas club accounts are designed to help you avoid last-minute financial stress by distributing your holiday savings over time. However, these accounts may come with restrictions and fees, so it's essential to review the terms and conditions before committing.

Traditional Savings Accounts

Another avenue is traditional savings accounts. Many financial institutions offer standard savings accounts that you can earmark for holiday spending. These accounts provide flexibility and ease of access, allowing you to contribute regularly and withdraw when needed. The right type of traditional savings account will ultimately depend on your financial strategy, initial deposit capability, and saving timeline.

Online-only Banks

Online banks and fintech platforms have introduced innovative options for holiday savings. Some offer automated savings features that round up your transactions to the nearest dollar, directing the spare change into your holiday fund. These micro-contributions can accumulate over time without requiring regular manual deposits. Additionally, some platforms offer higher interest rates, enhancing the growth potential of your holiday savings.

Setting Up Automatic Transfers

When it comes to achieving your financial goals, consistency is key. One powerful tool that can help you stay on track and build your savings effectively is setting up automatic transfers to your savings account. This simple yet impactful practice offers numerous benefits that can contribute to your financial well-being.

Ensures Consistency

Life can get busy, and it's easy to forget to manually transfer money to your savings account regularly. Automatic transfers eliminate this risk by scheduling recurring transfers on specific dates. This consistency in contributing to your savings rein-forces good financial habits and ensures that you're making progress toward your goals even during hectic times.

Prioritizes Savings

Automated transfers prioritize savings by treating them as non-negotiable expenses. Just like you wouldn't skip paying your rent or mortgage, automatic transfers make savings a top financial priority. This approach helps you build a strong financial foundation and reinforces the importance of saving for both short-term and long-term goals.

Reduces Temptation to Spend

When money sits in your checking account, it's easy to succumb to impulsive spending. By automatically transferring a portion of your income to your savings account, you create a buffer between your disposable income and your savings. This buffer makes it less likely for you to spend the money impulsively and increases the chances of it being saved for your intended purpose.

Removes Emotional Barriers

Saving money can sometimes be emotionally challenging, especially if it involves making conscious decisions to cut back on discretionary spending. Automatic transfers eliminate the need for constant decision-making and emotional hurdles. Once the transfer is set up, the money is saved without requiring daily mental effort, making it easier to stay committed to your financial goals.

Harnesses the Power of Compound Interest

Automating transfers means your savings consistently grow over time. The power of compound interest comes into play when your saved funds earn interest, and that interest earns even more interest. By setting up automatic transfers, you're allowing compound interest to work its magic more effectively and accelerate your savings growth.

Supports Long-Term Goals

Whether you're saving for a down payment on a home, a dream vacation, or retirement, consistency is vital. Automatic transfers ensure that you're steadily building your savings for the long term. It's a proactive approach to achieving your financial dreams without constantly monitoring and adjusting your savings contributions.

Minimizes Procrastination

Procrastination is a common barrier to financial success. It's easy to put off saving when you're caught up in day-to-day responsibilities. Automatic transfers eliminate the need for active decision-making, reducing the likelihood of procrastination. This way, your savings continue to grow even when you're preoccupied with other matters.

Creates a Sense of Financial Security

Having a consistent savings routine contributes to your overall financial security. Knowing that you're systematically building an emergency fund or saving for major expenses provides peace of mind. This sense of security can alleviate financial stress and allow you to focus on other aspects of your life.

Take Advantage Online Only Rewards

Many banks offer cash incentives just for making a certain amount of transactions or depositing a minimum amount as a promotion. You may reach your holiday savings goals by setting up a new account dedicated to the funds you need to automate. And as a bonus, you can continue to use the account in years to come.

Tips for Maximizing Automated Savings

Managing finances can be challenging, especially for individuals who struggle with budgeting and saving. Fortunately, automated savings can be a game-changer, offering a convenient way to build savings without constant monitoring.

Set Realistic Goals

Start by setting clear and achievable savings goals. Determine exactly what you're saving for. Break down your goals into smaller milestones, making it easier to track your progress and stay motivated.

Know Your Income and Expenses

Understanding your income and expenses is crucial for effective financial management. Review your monthly income and expenses for a few months to identify spending patterns. This will help you determine how much you can comfortably ration out to automated savings.

Create a Budget

A budget is a powerful tool that can help you control your spending and allocate funds to your savings goals. With the help of budgeting apps or spreadsheets, categorize your expenses and set limits for each category. Be sure to designate a portion of your income to savings as a non-negotiable expense.

Choose the Right Savings Account

Select a savings account that reflects with your goals. Look for accounts with no or low fees, competitive interest rates, and features that suit your needs. Online banks often offer higher yield savings accounts that can help your money grow faster than traditional banks.

Start Small and Gradually Increase

If you're new to automated savings, start with a modest amount that won't strain your budget. As you become more comfortable with the process, gradually increase the contribution. The key is to build consistency over time.

Schedule Transfers Strategically

Time your automated transfers with your pay schedule. Set them up shortly after your paycheck hits your account to ensure the money is saved before you have a chance to spend it.

Utilize Payroll Deductions

If your employer offers the option, set up automatic payroll deductions to divert a portion of your paycheck directly to your savings account. This "out of sight, out of mind" approach ensures that your savings contributions are made before you even see the money.

Match Transfers with Specific Goals

If you have multiple savings goals, create separate sub-accounts for each one. Allocate money accordingly to match your goals. For instance, if your holiday plans include saving for a vacation, label the sub-account as "Vacation Fund" and direct your automated transfers there.

Monitor and Adjust

While automated savings reduce the need for constant monitoring, it's essential to periodically review your progress. Check whether your savings contributions align with your goals and financial situation. Adjust the amounts if necessary to ensure you're staying on track.

Avoid Frequent Withdrawals

Resist the temptation to withdraw from your savings frequently. The purpose of automated savings is to build a safety net or achieve specific goals. Limit withdrawals to genuine emergencies or necessary fixed expenses to attain your goals.

Celebrate Milestones

When you reach savings milestones, celebrate your achievements. Treat yourself to a small reward or acknowledge your progress. Celebrating milestones can make the savings journey more enjoyable and motivating. Remember, consistency and patience are key, and over time, you'll see the positive impact on your savings and overall financial well-being.

Wrapping It All Up

Opening a savings account is a strategic move that offers a multitude of benefits beyond simply setting money aside. Savings accounts come in various forms, catering to different saving preferences and financial strategies. Christmas club accounts often involve depositing money throughout the year, with the bank releasing the accumulated funds in time for holiday spending. Traditional savings accounts can also be earmarked for holiday savings, offering flexibility and accessibility. Online banking platforms might provide innovative features like automated round-up contributions or higher interest rates.

Setting up automatic transfers to your savings account is a powerful financial strategy that offers a multitude of benefits. Start early as often as possible to maximize the benefits these accounts have to offer. From ensuring consistency and prioritizing savings to reducing the temptation to spend impulsively and harnessing the power of compound interest, this practice streamlines your journey to financial success. By harnessing these advantages, you're taking a proactive step toward enjoying a more financially balanced and joyful holiday season.

Smart Shopping Strategies

In today's fast-paced consumer-driven world, finding ways to stretch your hard-earned dollars further is crucial. Fortunately, the internet offers ways to not only build the money coming into your bank account, but also find the best way to minimize the amount leaving out of it. This chapter looks into the realm of smart shopping strategies, equipping you with a toolkit of techniques to make the most of your purchases and save money in the process.

Utilizing Price Comparison Tools

In the era of online shopping, price comparison tools have become indispensable allies for consumers seeking the best deals. These tools empower you to make informed purchasing decisions by providing a comprehensive view of prices across multiple retailers.

Online Platforms and Browser Extensions

Numerous online platforms and browser extensions are designed to simplify your shopping experience by comparing prices across various websites. One such tool is Honey, a browser extension that automatically scans the web for coupon codes and applies them to your cart, ensuring you get the best available price. CamelCamelCamel is another invaluable tool for Amazon shoppers, offering price tracking and historical data for products to help you identify optimal times to buy.

Mobile Apps

Mobile apps bring the power of price comparison right to your fingertips. Apps like ShopSavvy and PriceGrabber allow you to scan barcodes or search for products to instantly see prices from different retailers. This can be particularly useful when you're shopping in physical stores and want to ensure you're not missing out on online discounts.

Aggregator Websites

Aggregator websites compile prices from various online stores and present them in an easily digestible format. Websites like Google Shopping aggregate prices and show you where you can find the lowest cost for a specific item. These platforms often provide additional information such as nearby availability and similar products to help you make an informed decision.

Customized Alerts

Some price comparison tools offer the option to set up alerts for specific products. For instance, if you're eyeing a particular item but want to wait until it reaches a certain price, you can set up an alert. Once the price drops to your desired level, you'll receive a notification, allowing you to snag the deal.

In-Store Price Matching

Price comparison tools can also be used for in-store shopping. Many retailers offer price matching policies, where they match a lower price from a competitor's website. Armed with the information from your price comparison tool, you can confidently request a price match and secure the best deal without having to switch stores.

Reviews and Ratings

Price comparison tools often provide customer reviews and ratings alongside product listings. This insight can help you evaluate not only the cost but also the quality and performance of the item. Balancing price with value ensures you make purchases that complement your needs and expectations.

Avoiding Impulse Purchases

Perhaps one of the most significant benefits of price comparison tools is their ability to curb impulse purchases. By taking a moment to compare prices, you give yourself time to evaluate whether the purchase is truly necessary and whether you're getting the best deal available.

Staying Mindful of Shipping Costs

While price comparison tools focus on the product's cost, remember to factor in shipping fees when comparing prices across retailers. Sometimes, a slightly higher-priced item from one retailer may become more affordable when you consider free or lower shipping costs.

Shopping During Sales and Promotions

Strategically navigating sales and promotions is a key component of smart shopping. By capitalizing on discounts, special offers, and seasonal sales, you can stretch your holiday gift budget further without compromising on quality or quantity.

Stay Informed

Keeping an eye on upcoming sales and promotions is the first step. Subscribe to newsletters from your favorite retailers, follow them on social media, and download their mobile apps. Many stores announce exclusive sales and offer early access to loyal customers, giving you a head start on snagging the best deals.

Compare Prices

While sales and promotions can be exciting, don't assume that every discounted item is a great deal. Use price comparison tools to ensure that the discounted price is indeed lower than the regular price elsewhere. This extra step ensures you're truly saving money and not falling into the trap of a perceived bargain.

Stack Coupons and Discounts

Many retailers allow you to stack coupons on top of existing discounts. This can result in significant savings. For instance, if a store is offering a 20% off sale and you have a 10% off coupon, using both can result in a combined discount of 30%. Always check the retailer's coupon policy to understand how many discounts you can stack.

Loyalty Programs

Joining loyalty programs can grant you access to exclusive discounts and early sale previews. These programs often offer points for every purchase that can be redeemed for future discounts or rewards. Some stores also provide birthday discounts and personalized offers based on your shopping history.

Timing Is Key

Timing plays a crucial role in maximizing savings. While Black Friday and Cyber Monday are well-known sale events, consider shopping during mid-week sales, flash sales, and end-of-season clearance events. Retailers often reduce prices to move out old inventory, making it an excellent time to stock up on gifts for the upcoming year.

Research Return Policies

Before making a purchase during a sale or promotion, familiarize yourself with the retailer's return policy. Ensure that you can return or exchange items if they don't meet your expectations. This knowledge provides peace of mind and ensures you're not stuck with unwanted items.

Use Price Protection

Some credit cards offer price protection benefits that refund you the price difference if an item you purchased goes on sale shortly after your purchase. Check with your credit card provider to see if this benefit is available and how to take advantage of it.

Stay Organized

As you navigate different sales and promotions, it's easy to lose track of your purchases and the associated discounts. Keep a record of your purchases, including receipts, order confirmation emails, and discount codes. This helps you stay organized and ensures you're benefiting from the savings you've secured.

Cashback and Rewards Programs

Harnessing the power of cashback and rewards programs can significantly boost your savings when shopping for holiday gifts. These programs offer you a chance to earn back a portion of your spending in the form of cashback, points, or rewards. By strategically utilizing these programs, you can make your money work harder for you.

Choose the Right Programs: There are various cashback and rewards programs available, ranging from credit card rewards to standalone apps and browser extensions. Research and choose programs that align with your shopping habits and offer the most appealing benefits. Before joining any program, customers should review the program's terms, conditions, fee, and privacy policies to ensure they suit your preferences and values.

Credit Card Rewards: Many credit cards offer cashback or rewards for every purchase you make. These programs allow cardholders to earn various types of rewards, such as cash back, points, miles, or discounts, based on their spending behavior. To maximize the benefits of credit card rewards, it's crucial to choose a credit card that aligns with your spending habits and preferences. Consider whether any associated fees are worth the potential benefits.

Retailer Loyalty Programs: Retailers often have their own loyalty programs that offer exclusive discounts, early access to sales, and rewards for frequent purchases. Members may gain access to special events and product launches that are not available to regular customers. Some programs incorporate social media engagement, encouraging members to interact with the brand on social platforms for additional rewards. These rewards may include discounts, cash back, points, free products, personalized offers, and more.

Cashback Apps: Several apps, like Rakuten, Ibotta, and Honey, offer cashback on purchases made through their platforms. Before making a purchase, you just need to activate the cashback offer of your choice by clicking on it. Then make your purchase as you normally would, submit proof of purchase to the app, and withdraw your earnings once the purchase is verified. Usually you can withdraw to their bank account, PayPal, or even gift cards once the specified payout threshold has been reached. Some cashback apps provide exclusive offers that are only available to app users, giving them access to deals they wouldn't find elsewhere. Users can often earn extra cashback by referring friends and family to the app and take advantage of limited-time bonus cashback offers, especially during peak shopping seasons or holidays.

Browser Extensions: Browser extensions for cashback rewards are tools that users can install in their web browsers to automatically notify them of available cashback offers and discounts while they shop online. These extensions work by integrating with a cashback website or platform and providing real-time information about cashback opportunities, making you less likely to miss out on cashback offers because the extension detects and notifies them about opportunities. They make the process of earning cashback more seamless and convenient by eliminating the need to manually visit the cashback website and activate offers.

Stack and Combine Offers

One of the most effective strategies is stacking multiple offers. For example, use a cashback credit card to make a purchase through a cashback app while taking advantage of a retailer's loyalty program. This way, you can maximize your savings by earning rewards from multiple sources simultaneously.

Be Strategic with Credit Cards

If you're comfortable using credit cards responsibly, opt for cards that offer cashback or rewards for your most frequent purchases. Some cards offer higher cashback rates in specific categories like groceries, dining, or travel. Always pay off your credit card balance in full each month to avoid interest charges that can offset your rewards.

Redeem Wisely

When redeeming rewards, choose options that offer the most value. Cashback and statement credits are straightforward, while redeeming for gift cards or travel might provide enhanced value. Research redemption options and calculate their worth to ensure you're getting the best deal.

Utilize Sign-Up Bonuses

Many cashback and rewards programs offer sign-up bonuses for new members. These bonuses can provide a significant boost to your earnings, especially if you time your sign-up to coincide with major purchases.

Monitor Special Offers

Cashback and rewards programs often run special promotions, such as increased cashback rates for certain retailers or bonus points for specific purchases. Keep an eye out for these offers and adjust your shopping accordingly.

Be Mindful of Fees

Some rewards programs come with annual fees, especially premium credit cards that offer extensive benefits. Consider whether the fees are justified based on your spending habits and the rewards you'll earn. For no-annual-fee cards, the rewards you earn are essentially free money.

Read the Fine Print

Before signing up for any program, carefully read the terms and conditions. Understand how rewards are earned, when they expire, and any restrictions on redemption. Some programs might have blackout dates or limitations on how you can use your rewards.

Stay Consistent

To maximize your rewards, consistently use the cashback and rewards programs whenever you shop. The more you use them, the more you'll accumulate over time, enhancing your savings potential.

Stay Organized

Keep track of your rewards, cashback earnings, and redemption options. Set reminders for when rewards are set to expire so you don't miss out on valuable savings.

Bulk Buying to Save

When it comes to saving money on holiday gifts, bulk buying can truly give you more bang for your buck. Retailers and merchandisers will often reward wholesale purchases with discounts.

Identify Common Gifts

Start by identifying gifts that are versatile and suitable for multiple recipients. It enables you to maintain a well-stocked supply of presents that cater to a diverse range of recipients. Items like travel cups, chocolates, or small gadgets can often be purchased in larger quantities at a lower per-unit cost.This strategy not only allows you to take advantage of bulk pricing, thereby reducing the per-unit cost, but also ensures that you have a reserve of presents ready for unexpected occasions.

Compare Prices

Investing time into the research process to compare the cost of purchasing items individually versus in bulk is a strategic step that can significantly impact your holiday budget. Ensure that the bulk price per item is actually lower, taking into account not just the base cost but also any additional fees such as shipping or handling charges. Some retailers might offer free shipping for bulk orders, while others may have a small additional fee. Ensure that the overall cost, inclusive of these fees, still presents substantial savings compared to individual purchases.

Share with Others

Pooling resources with friends or family members to make bulk purchases is a savvy strategy that can unlock even more savings and make your holiday budget go even further. When negotiating group purchases, you might be eligible for enhanced discounts or preferential rates due to the larger quantity you're intending to purchase, so reach out to an individual business to inquire about any potential benefits. Determine the payment method, distribution plan, and other logistical details in advance. Technology can facilitate this process, as digital payment platforms allow for easy money transfer and coordination among group members.

Storage Considerations

Before committing to bulk purchases, it's essential to take a moment to evaluate your available storage space and how well it can handle the amount you plan to buy. Consider spaces such as closets, cabinets, underutilized corners, or even dedicated storage rooms if available. Take measurements of these spaces to determine their true capacity, if needed. Another consideration is the shelf life or expiration of items to avoid discarding expired items, negating the cost savings you initially gained.

Discounted Gift Cards for Budgeting

Discounted gift cards are a powerful tool for stretching your holiday shopping budget. These cards allow you to purchase items at a reduced cost, effectively providing you with instant savings.

Research Resale Marketplaces

Online platforms such as Raise, Cardpool, and Gift Card Granny provide a treasure trove of opportunities to access discounted gift cards, offering savvy shoppers a chance to maximize their savings while shopping for holiday gifts. Narrow down your search based on the specific retailers you're interested in and sort the results by discount percentage, card value, or other relevant criteria.

Stack with Other Offers

Take your money-saving strategy one step further by combining discounted gift cards with ongoing sales, promotions, and coupons. When planning your shopping trips, thoroughly research the upcoming sales events and promotions. Keep an eye out for Black Friday, Cyber Monday, end-of-season clearance sales, and other significant retail events. As you plan your shopping trips, prioritize items that are already on sale, have discounted prices, or are part of a promotion. Be sure to review the fine print before proceeding with your purchases.

Use for Big Purchases

If you have a high-ticket item on your gift list, consider using a discounted gift card to make the purchase. To illustrate, suppose you're eyeing a high-end electronic gadget that typically costs $800. If you manage to purchase a discounted gift card for the retailer with a 10% discount, you've already shaved off $80 from the total cost. Now, if that retailer happens to be running a seasonal sale with an additional 20% off, you'll be applying that discount to the already-reduced $720 amount, saving an additional $144. The cumulative savings from combining the discounted gift card with the ongoing sale brings your final purchase price down to just $576.

Electronic or Physical

Electronic gift cards, also known as e-gift cards, offer a level of convenience that is hard to match. These digital versions of traditional gift cards can be purchased and delivered almost instantly, eliminating the need for physical shipping and handling and making them an excellent option for last-minute gift-giving situations. This speed is particularly advantageous for time-sensitive occasions or spontaneous gift exchanges.

On the other hand, physical gift cards have their own set of advantages that make them a preferred choice for many individuals. They can be included in greeting cards or wrapped alongside other physical presents. Additionally, physical gift cards allow for more creative packaging and presentation, and may be a better option for younger loved ones who may not have access to a phone or a recipient who cannot access a printer and prefers a card they can hold in their hand.

Check Card Balance

Be sure that the gift card's balance matches the face value before using it for purchases. While most reputable platforms and sellers strive to provide accurate information, discrepancies can occasionally occur due to technical glitches or other factors. Retain any receipts, confirmation emails, or transaction records related to the purchase of the gift card. Before attempting to use the gift card, ensure that it has been properly activated.

Shopping Off-Season for Bargains

When it comes to smart shopping strategies, one of the most effective ways to save money on holiday gifts is by shopping off-season. By breaking away from the traditional holiday shopping rush, you can secure fantastic deals and bargains that would otherwise be unavailable.

Take Advantage of Clearance Sales

Many retailers offer clearance sales at the end of each season to make room for new inventory. For instance, winter clothing and gear tend to go on clearance as spring approaches. By shopping for holiday gifts during these clearance events, you can snag items at a fraction of their original cost.

Utilize Flash Sales and Special Events

Retailers often host flash sales, special events, and promotional days throughout the year. These occasions can provide excellent opportunities to find gifts at significantly reduced prices. Keep an eye on newsletters, social media, and retailer websites to stay informed about these events.

Consider Outlet Stores

Outlet stores are known for offering products from well-known brands at discounted prices. On top of the already steep discounts, these stores offer promotions and coupons throughout the year, so be sure to sign-up with their loyalty programs to maximize your savings. Often, you can find physical coupons at customer service or download an app to redeem the latest deals.

Look for Multi-Use Gifts

Items that can serve multiple purposes are perfect for off-season shopping. For example, kitchen gadgets, home decor, and accessories can be gifted during various occasions throughout the year, making them versatile options that can be purchased when they're on sale.

Shop Online Year-Round

Online retailers often offer deals and discounts that are not limited to specific seasons. By shopping online year-round, you can take advantage of lower prices, special promotions, and clearance events that might not be available in brick-and-mortar stores.

Stay Open to Gifting Options

Shopping off-season might require a level of flexibility when it comes to gift choices. Be open to considering alternative gifts that you might not have thought of initially. Exploring different options can lead to unique and thoughtful presents that fit your budget.

Combine Off-Season and DIY Gifts

If you're crafty, consider combining the off-season strategy with DIY gifts. For instance, you could buy discounted materials during off-season sales and use them to create personalized gifts that your loved ones will cherish.

Stay Mindful of Storage

While shopping off-season offers excellent savings, it's essential to consider storage space. Make sure you have adequate room to store your purchased items until the holiday season arrives.

Wrapping It All Up

Incorporating price comparison tools into your shopping routine can save you both time and money. Whether you're shopping for electronics, clothing, household essentials, or even booking travel, utilizing price comparison tools is an essential strategy for the modern consumer. With careful planning, comparison shopping, and a keen eye for discounts, you'll be able to find high-quality gifts at a fraction of the regular price, leaving you with extra funds to enjoy the holiday season to the fullest.

By mastering the art of shopping during sales and promotions, you can make the most of your holiday gift budget. Leveraging bulk buying and discounted gift cards, you can optimize your holiday shopping budget. By adopting the practice of shopping off-season, you're not only saving money but also avoiding the stress and rush that often accompany last-minute holiday shopping. With a little planning and an eye for deals, you can find the perfect gifts for your loved ones without compromising your budget.

Social Media and Price Alerts

The holiday season is a time of joy, celebration, and gift-giving. However, the expenses associated with purchasing gifts for friends and family can quickly add up, leaving many individuals feeling financially strained. Fortunately, the advent of technology and the rise of social media platforms have opened up new avenues for savvy shoppers to save money while still delighting their loved ones with thoughtful presents. This chapter will explore in detail how you can strategically use social media and sign up for price alerts to maximize your savings and make the most of your holiday gift budget.

Utilizing Social Media for Deals and Discounts

Social media platforms have evolved from mere channels of communication to treasure troves of deals and discounts. Brands, retailers, and influencers frequently use these platforms to engage with their audience by offering special promotions, exclusive codes, and limited-time offers. To tap into this potential, follow your favorite brands, retailers, and influencers on platforms like Facebook, Instagram, and X (formerly Twitter).

Following Your Favorite Brands and Retailers

Start by following the official pages of your preferred brands, retailers, and online stores. Many businesses use their social media platforms to announce flash sales, limited-time offers, and exclusive discounts available only to their followers. By staying connected, you ensure that you're among the first to know about these opportunities.

Engaging with Influencers and Bloggers

In addition to brands, influencers and bloggers often collaborate with companies to offer their followers special codes and promotions. These collaborations can lead to substantial savings on various products. Look for social media accounts that match your interests, and keep an eye out for posts promoting exclusive offers.

Participating in Contests and Giveaways

Many brands and influencers organize contests and giveaways on social media as a way to engage with their audience and gain exposure. Participating in these activities can not only be fun but also provide a chance to win free products or receive special discount codes as prizes.

Joining Facebook Groups and Communities

Facebook Groups dedicated to frugal living, bargain hunting, and specific interests can be treasure troves of money-saving information. Members often share their discoveries, tips, and strategies for finding the best deals. Search for relevant groups in your area to become part of an active community focused on savings.

Utilizing Hashtags for Deal Discovery

On platforms like Instagram and X, hashtags are powerful tools for discovering deals. Search for hashtags related to discounts, such as #deals, #sale, #discounts, or even specific product-related hashtags. This can lead you to posts from both brands and individuals sharing information about ongoing promotions.

Turning on Post Notifications

For brands and accounts that consistently share deals and discounts, consider turning on post notifications. This way, you'll receive instant alerts whenever they publish a new post or offer. This can be especially helpful during limited-time sales events.

Creating a Separate Shopping Account

If you're concerned about your main social media feed getting cluttered with promotional posts, consider creating a separate account specifically for following brands, retailers, and influencers. In doing so, your main account remains focused on personal connections while your shopping account keeps you up to date with savings opportunities.

Engaging with Interactive Posts

Some brands create interactive posts like polls, quizzes, and challenges to engage with their audience. These posts often come with the reward of discount codes or exclusive offers for participants when they like, comment, and share a post. Keep an eye out for such interactive content and participate to reap the benefits.

Following Brands and Influencers for Exclusive Offers

Social media has become a vibrant marketplace where brands and influencers collaborate to offer exclusive deals and promotions to their followers. By strategically following these accounts, you can access special offers that aren't always available through traditional channels.

Identify Relevant Brands and Influencers

Start by identifying brands and influencers that align with your interests and preferences. Whether you're looking into fashion, technology, beauty, or niche hobbies, there are likely accounts that cater to your preferences. Look for accounts that frequently share discounts or promotional codes.

Explore Instagram and Facebook Stories

Many brands and influencers use the "Stories" feature on platforms like Instagram and Facebook to share time-sensitive deals. These stories often include swipe-up links that take you directly to the discounted product or offer. Since Stories disappear after 24 hours, this is a great way to catch limited-time deals.

Subscribe to Newsletters and Emails

Once you've found brands or influencers whose offers you value, consider subscribing to their newsletters or email updates. This quick step will allow you to receive notifications about upcoming sales, exclusive offers, and new product launches directly in your inbox.

Look for Collaborations and Partnerships

Influencers frequently collaborate with brands to offer their followers special deals. Keep an eye out for posts that mention collaborations or partnerships, as these often come with unique discount codes that you can use at checkout.

Participate in Giveaways

Influencers often host giveaways in partnership with brands. Participating in these giveaways not only gives you a chance to win products but also often leads to discovering new brands and their associated discounts. Follow with post notifications on to make sure you don't miss out on these contests.

Check Stories Highlights

Many influencers save their Stories as highlights on their profile. These highlights often include valuable information, such as discount codes, that you can access even after the initial story has expired.

Be Mindful of Authenticity

While following brands and influencers for exclusive offers can be rewarding, it's essential to verify the authenticity of the accounts you engage with. Stick to well-known brands, reputable influencers, and accounts that have a history of providing legitimate deals.

Setting Up Price Alerts and Notifications

As outlined in the last chapter, harnessing the power of technology to track price drops and special offers can be a game-changer when it comes to saving money on your holiday gifts. Price alerts and notifications allow you to stay informed about price changes and discounts without constantly monitoring websites. Social media even allows you to view and share wish lists to take the guesswork out of which gifts to buy, invaluable for finding exactly what your recipient wants and joint gifting responsibilities.

Monitor Social Media Accounts

Brands and retailers occasionally share flash sales, limited-time promotions, and discount codes on their social media accounts. By following them on platforms like X and Facebook, you can stay updated on these offers and potentially snag deals before they expire.

Use Deal Aggregator Websites

Deal aggregator websites compile various deals, discounts, and offers from different retailers in one place. Websites like Slickdeals and RetailMeNot offer a wealth of information on ongoing sales and promotions.

Customize Your Notifications

When setting up price alerts, make sure to customize your notifications to avoid being overwhelmed by excessive alerts. Choose specific criteria, such as the percentage of price drop or the specific products you're interested in.

Be Ready to Act

Price drops and promotions can be time-sensitive, so it's essential to be ready to make a purchase when you receive an alert. Ensure that the item is still within your budget and goes with your needs before making a decision.

Engaging in Online Communities for Tips and Insights

The digital age has ushered in a wealth of online communities where like-minded individuals gather to share their experiences, insights, and tips. When it comes to finding the best deals, discounts, and strategies for saving money on holiday gifts, these communities can be a goldmine of valuable information.

Join Social Media Groups

Platforms like Facebook and Reddit host a multitude of groups dedicated to deal hunting, frugal living, and budget-friendly shopping. Search for groups relevant to your interests, such as "Holiday Deals and Discounts" or "Frugal Gift Ideas," and join them to participate in discussions and gain insights from fellow members.

Participate in Forums

Online forums have been around for decades and remain a hub of knowledge sharing. Websites like FatWallet, Slickdeals, and The Money Mustache Community have vibrant forums where users discuss various ways to save money, including finding the best holiday gift deals.

Follow Niche Bloggers and Influencers

Many personal finance bloggers and social media influencers specialize in finding and sharing money-saving strategies. Follow them on platforms like Instagram, X, and YouTube to access their latest tips and recommendations for scoring great deals during the holiday season.

Utilize Hashtags

On social media platforms like Instagram and Twitter, hashtags like #BlackFridayDeals, #HolidaySavings, and #FrugalGiftIdeas can lead you to posts and discussions centered around finding budget-friendly gifts and deals.

View Webinars and Live Streams

Some online communities offer webinars and some form of live videos focused on money-saving techniques and shopping strategies. Participating in these virtual events can provide you with actionable tips and insights from experts in the field.

Share Your Own Discoveries

Online communities thrive on the exchange of information. If you come across a fantastic deal or a unique way to save money, don't hesitate to share it with the community. Your contribution could help others save money too.

Ask Questions

If you're unsure about a certain deal or you're looking for advice on finding specific gifts, don't hesitate to ask questions within these communities. Members are usually more than willing to share their experiences and offer guidance.

Stay Updated

Online communities can be fast-paced, and information can change rapidly. Make it a habit to check in regularly to stay updated on the latest deals, discounts, and insights shared by fellow members.

Verify Information

While online communities can be a valuable source of information, it's essential to verify any information or deals before making a purchase. Check multiple sources and reviews to ensure that you're making informed decisions.

Wrapping It All Up

By strategically utilizing social media, you can turn your scrolling time into a productive venture for finding deals and discounts on holiday gifts. Keep in mind that while social media can be a valuable resource, it's important to exercise caution and verify the authenticity of offers before making a purchase. With a discerning eye and a willingness to explore, you can unlock a world of savings through your social media feeds.

When you curate your social media feed to include brands and influencers that prioritize sharing exclusive offers, you can create a personalized shopping experience that caters to your preferences and helps you save money on your holiday gifts. Setting up price alerts and notifications can help you stay informed about the best deals and discounts without dedicating excessive time to monitoring prices manually. This technology-driven approach empowers you to make well-informed purchasing decisions and save money on your holiday gifts.

Part-Time Jobs and Side Gigs

The holiday season is a time of joy and giving, but it can also be a time of increased expenses. If you're looking to supplement your income and make the most of your holiday budget, exploring part-time jobs and side gigs can be an effective strategy. This chapter is all about showing you various ways you can earn extra money to enhance your holiday celebrations.

Exploring Temporary Job Opportunities

The holiday season is a time when businesses experience a surge in demand, making it an ideal opportunity to explore temporary job opportunities. These short-term positions not only offer a chance to earn extra income but also allow you to immerse yourself in the festive atmosphere.

Retail and Customer Service

Retail stores, malls, and department stores are bustling with shoppers during the holiday season. Temporary positions as sales associates, cashiers, or customer service representatives are often available. Keep in mind the potential to earn extra income with companies that offer additional incentives in the form of increased pay during the holiday season and bonuses for signing customers up to specific promotions and programs.

Seasonal Event Staff

The holidays bring a slew of events, from holiday markets to winter carnivals. Event organizers often hire temporary staff to help with event setup, ticketing, crowd management, and providing information to attendees. Many holiday events occur during evenings and weekends, making event-related positions ideal for individuals with existing commitments during regular working hours.

Package Delivery

With the rise of online shopping, package delivery services like Amazon Flex and UPS hire seasonal drivers to manage the influx of orders. This role involves delivering packages to customers' doorsteps and ensuring timely deliveries. If you're comfortable driving and have a reliable vehicle, this could be a flexible way to earn extra income. Strive to provide excellent service to receive positive reviews, which can lead to more opportunities and higher earnings.

Hospitality and Catering

Holiday parties, corporate events, and family gatherings are common during this time. Catering companies and event venues often seek temporary staff to assist with serving food, managing buffets, and ensuring the event runs smoothly. Remember that there are also opportunities during other times of the year, such as weddings, conferences, and birthdays. By gaining experience and establishing connections during the holiday season, you might open doors to year-round event work to fuel your savings income.

Holiday Attractions

Many cities set up holiday attractions such as ice skating rinks, Christmas tree lots, and festive pop-up markets. These attractions not only spread holiday cheer but also create opportunities for temporary employment, often requiring additional staff to handle admissions, skate rentals, and sales of holiday goods. By working at holiday attractions, you immerse yourself in the festive atmosphere, and create a unique and heartwarming work environment.

Freelancing and Gig Economy Platforms

In the digital age, freelancing and gig economy platforms have revolutionized the way people earn income. These platforms offer a plethora of opportunities to leverage your skills and expertise to earn money on your own terms. During the holiday season, these platforms can be particularly valuable for boosting your savings for gifts and expenses.

Identify Your Skills

Take stock of your skills, talents, and expertise. Don't discount your abilities. No matter your level of mastery, there's likely a demand for your skills on freelancing platforms. Bear in mind, customers may be looking for someone to perform a task that is beyond their capability. Other times, they are looking for someone to provide them a service that will simply save them time.

Writing and Content Creation: If you have a way with words, consider offering your services as a freelance writer or content creator. Content is in high demand across industries, including blog posts, articles, web content, social media posts, and even e-books. Your ability to craft engaging and informative content can be a valuable asset to businesses and individuals seeking to enhance their online presence.

Graphic Design and Visual Arts: Graphic designers and artists are sought after for various design projects, such as creating logos, branding materials, social media graphics, illustrations, and infographics. Your artistic flair can help businesses and clients communicate their message effectively through eye-catching designs.

Programming and Web Development: Nowadays, programming and web development skills are highly valuable. You can offer services such as website development, app creation, coding, and software development. Businesses and entrepreneurs often require these skills to establish or enhance their online platforms.

Photography and Videography: If you have a knack for capturing moments through a lens, freelance photography and videography might be ideal for you. Individuals and companies frequently require professional photographs and videos for marketing, events, product launches, and more.

Social Media Management: If you're savvy with social media platforms, consider becoming a freelance social media manager. Many businesses struggle to maintain an active and engaging online presence, and your expertise in managing social media accounts and creating compelling content can make a significant impact.

Language and Translation Services: Fluency in multiple languages can open doors to freelance opportunities in translation, transcription, and language tutoring. Businesses looking to expand globally often require translation services for their content.

Virtual Assistance: Virtual assistants offer administrative and organizational support to busy professionals and entrepreneurs. Tasks can include scheduling appointments, managing emails, data entry, and more. Your organizational skills and attention to detail can be invaluable in this role.

Online Tutoring and Teaching: If you excel in a particular subject or have expertise in a certain area, online tutoring or teaching could be a rewarding gig. Many online platforms connect educators with students seeking to enhance their skills and knowledge.

Music and Art: If you're a musician or artist, platforms that offer commission-based art or custom music composition can be a great fit. From jingles for advertisements to custom artwork, your creative talents can find a niche in various projects.

Consulting and Coaching: If you're an expert in a specific field, consider offering consulting or coaching services. Whether it's business, finance, career development, fitness, or personal growth, your guidance and expertise can help individuals achieve their goals.

Event Planning and Coordination: If you're organized and detail-oriented, freelance event planning and coordination can be an exciting venture. From weddings to corporate events, your ability to create memorable experiences can be in high demand.

Health and Wellness Services: If you're a certified fitness instructor, nutritionist, or wellness coach, you can offer your services online. Virtual fitness classes, personalized meal plans, and wellness coaching are just a few ways to use your expertise to help others.

Accounting and Financial Services: If you have a background in accounting or finance, you can offer services such as bookkeeping, financial analysis, tax preparation, and budgeting assistance to individuals and businesses.

Research and Data Analysis: Strong research and analytical skills are highly sought after in various industries. Businesses often require research reports, market analysis, and data interpretation to make informed decisions.

Market Research

Research the demand for your chosen skill or hobby. Delve into the market to understand the needs and preferences of potential customers, ensuring that there's a viable audience willing to pay for the services you're planning to offer. Join online forums, social media groups, and communities related to your skill or hobby. Look for gaps and unaddressed pain points to find areas where you can offer something unique. Highlight these distinctive selling points in your marketing.

Explore Platforms

There are numerous freelancing platforms like Upwork, Fiverr, and Freelancer where clients post projects and tasks they need assistance with. Whether you're looking to showcase your creative talents, leverage your professional skills, or share your expertise, freelancing platforms offer a diverse range of opportunities. Browse through the listings to find projects that match up with your abilities. Consider researching platforms that align with your expertise for a more targeted approach.

Create a Profile

Setting up a compelling profile on freelancing platforms is essential. Your freelancing profile serves as your digital portfolio and first impression. Craft an eye-catching profile that highlights your skills, experience, and past projects. Clients often use profiles to assess whether you're a good fit for their projects. A well-crafted one increases your chances of attracting clients.

Bid Wisely

When bidding on projects, take the time to craft personalized and well-written proposals. Address the client's needs, explain how you can add value, and showcase your understanding of the project by carefully reading the project description and requirements. Tailor your proposals for each job to demonstrate your genuine interest and commitment.

Deliver Quality Work

Approach freelance work with the same level of professionalism you would in a traditional job. Timely and high-quality work is key to building a positive reputation on freelancing platforms. Focus on delivering exceptional work and excellent customer service to earn glowing reviews from satisfied clients. Be responsive, meet deadlines, and go the extra mile to exceed expectations. Satisfied clients are more likely to provide positive reviews and recommend you to others.

Set Realistic Rates

While it's important to price your services competitively, don't undervalue your skills. Consider offering different packages or tiers to cater to various client needs and budgets. Discuss project details, expectations, timelines, and payment terms with clients upfront. Address any questions or concerns promptly and maintain open lines of communication throughout the project. Research the market rates for your services and set a price that reflects your expertise.

Time Management

Freelancing offers a remarkable degree of flexibility, but effective time management is crucial. Use the technique of time blocking to grant specific time slots for different tasks. Leverage productivity tools like calendar apps, task management software, and time-tracking tools can help you monitor your progress and identify areas for improvement. Balance your freelancing work with your other commitments to ensure you meet deadlines and maintain a healthy work-life balance.

Expand Your Services

As you embark on your freelancing journey, it's wise to start with smaller projects to gain experience and build a track record. Once you've built up your reputation, consider expanding your skill set to increase your marketability. Learning new tools, software, or techniques relevant to your field can open doors to a wider range of projects. The more versatile you are, the more opportunities you can explore.

Networking

Building relationships with clients can lead to repeat business and referrals. Maintain open communication and professionalism to foster positive relationships. Participate in forums, webinars, and groups related to your field. Engaging with other freelancers can provide a sense of community and access to shared knowledge. Connections within this industry can lead to future opportunities and potential recommendations for roles not advertised to the general public.

Offer Workshops or Classes

If you're skilled in a particular craft or activity, consider offering workshops or classes. Decide whether your workshops will be in-person, virtual, or a blend of both. Keep participants engaged during the workshop through interactive activities, discussions, and practical exercises. Clearly outline the content, objectives, and benefits of each workshop in your promotional materials. Prepare visually appealing handouts, guides, or presentations to complement your workshop content.

Start a Blog or YouTube Channel

Share your knowledge through a blog or YouTube channel. This can attract a following and generate income through ads, sponsorships, and affiliate marketing. Focus on providing high-quality content that adds value to your audience. Respond to questions, acknowledge feedback, and foster a sense of community around your content. Building a substantial following and generating income takes time. Don't be discouraged by slow initial growth. Consistency and persistence will pay off in the long term.

Social Media Marketing

Use social media platforms to showcase your skills, connect with potential clients, and establish your brand presence. Share testimonials from satisfied clients to provide social proof of your skills and can influence potential clients to trust your expertise. Host live sessions where you can interact with your audience in real-time. Maintain a regular posting schedule to keep your audience engaged and informed.

Sell Your Creations

If you're skilled in crafting, consider selling handmade products online. Platforms like Etsy provide a well-known marketplace for handmade goods. Write clear and engaging product descriptions. Use keywords relevant to your niche to improve search visibility. Calculate the cost of materials, your time, and overhead expenses to set competitive yet profitable prices. Consider selling digital products to further reduce costs.

Plan Ahead

As the holiday season approaches, it's important to be proactive and anticipate the surge in demand for specific services. Prioritize projects that are a good fit for your skills and have the potential to provide a substantial return on investment. Allow some buffer time in your schedule to accommodate unexpected delays or changes. Be prepared to adjust your strategy if circumstances change.

Balancing Work with Holiday Preparations

As you embark on part-time jobs or side gigs to boost your holiday savings, it's crucial to find a balance between your work commitments and the preparations for the holiday season. Juggling work, personal life, and holiday preparations can be challenging, but with effective planning and time management, you can make the most of both worlds.

Create a Schedule

Craft a weekly or monthly schedule that outlines when you'll dedicate time to freelancing projects, client communication, administrative tasks, and personal commitments on a calendar. Having a visual representation of your commitments helps you divvy up time efficiently without feeling overwhelmed. Utilize productivity apps, task managers, and calendars to keep track of your schedule and deadlines.

Set Priorities

Determine your priorities for both work and holiday preparations. Create a to-do list or use task management tools to prioritize your tasks. Identify the most urgent and important tasks and allocate sufficient time for each. This helps you stay focused and organized, ensuring that you meet your deadlines.

Break Down Tasks

Divide your holiday preparations into smaller, manageable tasks. Assign specific tasks to different days or weeks to avoid feeling overwhelmed. Breaking down tasks allows you to tackle them one step at a time, making the workload seem more achievable and reduces the likelihood of procrastination.

Set Realistic Goals

Communicate with clients, colleagues, and family members about your availability and the time you can realistically dedicate to various tasks. Setting clear expectations prevents misunderstandings and allows others to plan accordingly. Avoiding overcommitment helps prevent burnout and ensures that you can maintain a healthy balance between your professional and personal responsibilities.

Batch Similar Tasks

Group similar tasks together to help you streamline your workflow during the busy holiday season. Employ batch processing, which involves tackling similar tasks consecutively, which helps minimize context switching and optimizes your concentration. For instance, when wrapping gifts, wrap all of them at once rather than doing a few here and there.

Delegate When Possible

If you have family members or roommates, delegate some holiday tasks to share the workload. Allow everyone to express their preferences and strengths so that tasks align with individual capabilities. Use the opportunity to share family or cultural traditions associated with the holidays while also making the holiday season more enjoyable and memorable for everyone involved.

Take Breaks

Don't underestimate the importance of breaks. Incorporating well-timed breaks into your schedule can help you recharge, refocus, and approach tasks with renewed energy. Stepping away from tasks for a short period allows your brain to recover, which ultimately enhances your overall productivity and prevent burnout.

Learn to Say No

While the allure of taking on extra work to boost your savings is enticing, it's crucial to strike a balance between your financial goals and your overall well-being, especially during the holiday season. Politely declining additional commitments that could potentially hinder your holiday preparations ensures that you maintain a healthy equilibrium and prioritize both your financial objectives and the enjoyment of the festive season.

Stay Organized

Keep your workspace and living area organized to minimize distractions and increase focus when working or preparing for the holidays. Designate specific areas for work and holiday preparations and maintain these areas on a regular basis. Clutter and disarray can lead to distractions and a sense of chaos, which can impede your ability to stay on top of both work commitments and holiday tasks.

Communicate with Clients or Employers

If you're freelancing or working part-time, communicate your availability and potential downtime to clients or employers in advance. Even if you're taking time off for the holidays, maintain professionalism in your communication. Respond to messages promptly, and if you're completely unavailable, inform clients or employers about your return date. Clear communication minimizes misunderstandings and allows you to enjoy your holiday preparations without compromising your work commitments.

Practice Self-Care

Amidst the hustle and bustle, don't forget to take care of yourself. A crucial aspect of effective time management is taking care of yourself. Prioritize self-care through exercise, getting enough sleep, eat well, and engaging in activities that bring you joy. Addressing your needs alongside your responsibilities actually enhances your ability to manage your time effectively. By incorporating these practices into your daily routine, you create a strong foundation for juggling the holiday tasks and commitments while maintaining your well-being.

Celebrate Small Wins

Acknowledge and celebrate your accomplishments as an essential part of maintaining motivation and a positive mindset in the middle of the holiday rush. When you achieve even small milestones, take a moment to acknowledge your efforts and the progress you've made. Remember, celebrating your achievements isn't about grand gestures; it's about acknowledging the effort you put in and the progress you're making. These moments of recognition create a positive feedback loop that propels you forward, boosts your confidence, and maintains your enthusiasm throughout the holiday season's demands.

Wrapping It All Up

When exploring temporary job opportunities, keep in mind that communication and flexibility are crucial. Temporary positions may have varying schedules and require adapting to different roles and responsibilities. Additionally, these roles provide a chance to experience the holiday spirit firsthand and interact with people in a festive environment.

Freelancing and gig economy platforms provide a flexible and convenient way to earn extra income, especially during the holiday season. Whether you're looking to earn a little extra for gifts or save for holiday expenses, these platforms offer a range of opportunities that cater to various skills and interests. Effectively marketing your skills, delivering quality work, and maintaining professionalism can leverage freelancing to enhance your financial resources during the holidays.

Balancing work commitments with holiday preparations requires effective time management, clear priorities, and self-care. By creating a well-structured schedule, setting realistic goals, and maintaining a healthy work-life balance, you can excel in both your income-generating efforts and your holiday preparations. Remember that the holiday season is meant to be enjoyed, so finding harmony between work and festivities is key to making the most of this special time of year.

DIY and Homemade Gifts

The thought and effort that go into creating do-it-yourself (DIY) and homemade gifts stand out as genuine expressions of love and care. These unique creations carry with them the thoughtfulness and effort that embody true expressions of love and care. The beauty of crafting personalized presents lies not only in the budget-friendly aspect but in the depth of emotions they evoke. This chapter guides you through the techniques, ideas, and inspirations that will help you transform ordinary materials into extraordinary gifts filled with sentimental value.

Embracing the Beauty of Homemade Gifts

While today's world is often characterized by mass production and consumerism, the value of homemade gifts stands as a refreshing and meaningful alternative. These gifts offer a range of benefits that extend far beyond their aesthetic appeal.

Uniqueness and Exclusivity

One of the most compelling benefits of homemade gifts is their inherent uniqueness. Unlike store-bought items that are replicated thousands of times, your homemade creation is a one-of-a-kind masterpiece. This exclusivity adds a touch of luxury to the gift, making the recipient feel truly special.

Emotional Connection and Memories

The act of making a homemade gift involves more than just the physical materials; it carries emotional significance. As you work on the gift, you may reminisce about shared memories, experiences, and moments you have with the recipient. This process infuses the gift with sentimental value, turning it into a vessel of cherished memories.

Tailored to Fit Any Budget

Homemade gifts offer the flexibility to match your budget while still creating something remarkable. By sourcing materials economically and leveraging your skills, you can produce a gift that appears far more valuable than its dollar cost. This budget-friendly approach allows you to focus on the thought and effort behind the gift rather than its monetary value.

Environmental and Sustainable Choice

As sustainability is gaining increasing importance, homemade gifts go hand in hand with eco-conscious values. By creating your gifts, you have more control over the materials you use, ensuring that they are ethically sourced and environmentally friendly. Additionally, the reduction in mass-produced items can contribute to a decrease in waste and promote a more sustainable lifestyle.

Expression of Creativity

Homemade gifts provide a canvas for your creativity to flourish. Whether you're an experienced crafter or a novice, the process of creating a gift allows you to express yourself artistically. Your unique touch and creativity are showcased in every detail, making the gift a true representation of your personality and talents.

DIY Gift Ideas

Crafting your own gifts offers a world of possibilities for expressing your creativity and showing your loved ones how much you care. Your choice to invest time and energy in crafting a gift speaks volumes about the value you place on your relationship. These handmade treasures are not mere objects; they are tokens of your affection, creativity, and the sentiment you pour into every facet of their design.

Handmade Candles

Create a cozy ambiance with handmade candles. Begin by selecting high-quality wax, such as soy, beeswax, or paraffin, known for their clean-burning properties. Experiment with scents, ranging from soothing lavender and invigorating citrus to comforting vanilla and earthy sandalwood. Use color by incorporating natural dyes or candle-safe colorants to achieve the desired shade. Enhance the personal touch of your candles by customizing the containers made of glass jars, rustic tin, or even repurposed vintage teacups.

Handwritten Letters and Notes

In the middle of constant digital communication, a handwritten letter or a collection of heartfelt notes holds a special charm. It's never an inappropriate time to let someone know that you are thinking of them. Pour your thoughts onto paper, expressing gratitude, sharing memories, or offering words of encouragement. Presentation will only elevate this sort of gift. Consider using a decorative card stock or framing your paper to add an extra special touch.

Photo Memory Book

Capture cherished memories in a photo memory book. Compile pictures, mementos, and heartfelt notes to create a unique keepsake that celebrates your relationship and shared experiences. Incorporate your creativity by playing with layouts, backgrounds, and design elements. Many online platforms offer user-friendly templates that allow you to create a polished and professional-looking gift.

Customized Jewelry

Crafting your own jewelry allows you to tailor each piece to the recipient's style. Design personalized necklaces, bracelets, or earrings using beads, charms, and other materials. Consider adding birthstones or initials to make it even more special. Ultimately, the gift of handmade jewelry transcends its aesthetic appeal.

Homemade Spa Products

Treat your loved ones to a spa experience at home with homemade bath salts, scrubs, and body butters. Package them in decorative jars and label them with relaxing names like "Pampering Lavender." Enhance them by infusing essential oils like lavender, chamomile, or eucalyptus, known for their calming and aromatic properties. Incorporate dried flowers, to add a visually appealing touch. Present your handmade bath products in a beautiful gift basket.

Hand-Painted Mugs

Transform plain mugs into personalized works of art with hand-painted designs. Whether you're skilled at painting intricate patterns or prefer simple brushstrokes, each mug will carry your artistic flair. Adding details like names, initials, or special dates can make your mugs even more personal. Complement your mugs with coordinating coasters, hot cocoa mix, or a selection of artisan teas for a charming and complete package.

Infused Olive Oils or Vinegars

Delight the taste buds of your food-loving friends and family members with a personalized culinary gift. For an added touch of elegance, source decorative glass bottles that showcase various colors and textures. Include cards with suggestions for incorporating the infused flavors into salads, marinades, pasta dishes, and more that will remind them of the special effort you put into curating a gift that elevates their culinary experiences.

Knitted or Crocheted Accessories

If you have knitting or crocheting skills, tap into the world of cozy warmth and timeless fashion by creating handmade pieces that will keep them warm during the colder months. Incorporating their favorite colors or creating a color palette that complements their wardrobe can make the accessory even more special. These items are perfect for recipients that prioritize function and sustainability.

Custom Recipe Book

Compile family recipes, secret ingredients, and cooking tips into a custom recipe book. Alongside the recipes, share stories about the origins of each dish or the memories associated with them. While you may choose to create a physical recipe book, consider offering a digital version as well.

Personalized Wall Art

Design and create personalized wall art that reflects their passions and interests. Whether it's a painted canvas, a string art piece, or a framed quote, this gift will add a unique touch to their living space. Gather inspiration from free generative art tools and social media. The beauty of personalized wall art lies not only in its aesthetic appeal but also in its ability to tell a story, spark conversations, and evoke emotions for years to come.

Crafting on a Budget

Crafting homemade gifts doesn't have to break the bank. With a little creativity and resourcefulness, you can create meaningful and impressive DIY gifts without overspending.

Dollar Stores and Discount Shops

Dollar stores and discount shops are treasure troves for budget-friendly crafting supplies. You can find a wide range of items such as ribbon, beads, paints, brushes, and even blank canvases. Keep an eye out for seasonal decorations and themed items that can add a unique touch to your creations without straining your wallet. Remember these stores are constantly updating their inventory, so frequent visits can yield new and inspiring materials for your crafting projects.

Thrift Stores and Secondhand Shops

Thrift stores are fantastic places to discover hidden gems. Look for gently-used picture frames, fabrics, buttons, and other craft-worthy materials. You can repurpose these items to create entirely new and unique gifts. Inspect the shelves for ceramic or glass items that can be transformed with a bit of paint or embellishment.

Online Marketplaces

Online marketplaces like eBay, Etsy, and Amazon offer a variety of affordable crafting supplies right at your fingertips. Additionally, online platforms often have a wide selection of unique and niche materials that may not be available in local stores. When exploring these online marketplaces, take advantage of features like price comparison tools and seller history to ensure you're getting the best deal on your chosen supplies.

Recycling and Upcycling

Before you toss something in the recycling bin, consider whether it can be repurposed for crafting. Old magazines, newspapers, cardboard boxes, and glass jars can be transformed into creative and eco-friendly gifts. Upcycling not only saves money but also helps reduce waste. Look around your home for items that can be repurposed for crafting. Old clothes, fabrics, buttons, and jewelry can be deconstructed and transformed into new creations.

Sales and Clearance Sections

Keep an eye on sales and clearance sections in craft stores. Often, items that are slightly outdated or have minor imper- fections are available at significantly reduced prices. Consider how you can use these materials in unexpected ways to create something that stands out and showcases your vision. Keep a list of your upcoming projects and their requirements in mind while browsing the sales and clearance sections so you can snag items that go with your crafting plans and make the best purchases.

Borrowing or Swapping Supplies

If you're working on a specific project that requires tools or materials you don't have, consider borrowing from friends or family members who share your crafting interests. You can also participate in crafting groups or online platforms where members exchange or lend supplies. Some libraries or community centers offer materials like sewing machines, tools, and even specialty craft items for members to borrow, allowing access to what you need without purchasing it outright.

Nature and Free Materials

Nature provides a wealth of free crafting materials. Leaves, twigs, pinecones, and shells can be used to create beautiful and rustic decor. Before incorporating natural materials into your crafts, give them a gentle cleaning to remove dirt, insects, or debris. Just make sure to gather responsibly and respect local regulations when collecting natural materials. Don't hesitate to combine natural elements with other crafting supplies.

Personalizing Gifts

The beauty of DIY and homemade gifts lies not just in their uniqueness but in the personal touch you can add to each creation. When you personalize a gift, you're showing the recipient that you've put time, effort, and thought into crafting something specifically for them. Whether you're a seasoned crafter or trying DIY for the first time, adding a personal touch to your gifts is a rewarding endeavor that spreads joy and appreciation.

Consider the Recipient's Interests

Before you start crafting, take some time to think about the recipient's interests, hobbies, and preferences. What do they enjoy doing in their free time? What are their favorite colors, patterns, or styles? Have they mentioned any specific items they wish they had or themes they resonate with? Tailor your gift to align with what they love.

Add Their Name or Initials

Incorporate the recipient's name or initials into the gift design. You can embroider their name on a towel, engrave it on a piece of jewelry, or paint it onto a canvas. Merge functionality and personalization by adding their name to items they use daily that not only serves a purpose but also becomes a part of their everyday routine.

Design Practical Gifts with a Twist

Create practical gifts with a personalized twist. For instance, if you're crafting a kitchen apron, sew on pockets with fabric patterns related to the recipient's hobbies. If you're making a tote bag, choose a design that reflects their personal interests.

By infusing these thoughtful details into your practical DIY creations, you're crafting gifts that go beyond functionality.

Package Thoughtfully

The presentation of the gift can also add a personalized touch. Use the recipient's favorite coloring to wrap their present. On the other hand, you could step away from traditional wrapping paper and consider using unconventional materials. Craft paper, maps, old book pages, or fabric remnants can all add a distinct and charming element to the presentation to make the unwrapping experience even more special.

Wrapping It All Up

The benefits of homemade gifts go beyond money. They tap into the emotional aspects of giving, allowing you to express love, care, and thoughtfulness in a tangible form. The unique nature of these gifts, their personalized touch, and the emotional connection they foster make them treasured keepsakes that will be remembered and cherished for years to come. While exploring budget-friendly options, you'll be able to create thoughtful and impressive DIY gifts without overspending. Remember that crafting is about creativity, and sometimes unique materials can lead to extraordinary creations.

DIY and homemade gifts have the power to strengthen relationships, convey emotions, and showcase your creativity.

By embracing the benefits of homemade gifts, exploring diverse DIY ideas, being resourceful with crafting materials, and adding personalized elements, you'll create presents that leave a lasting impact on those you care about. These gifts are more than just items; they're tangible expressions of love and thoughtfulness that will be cherished for years to come.

Planning for Next Year's Gifts

As one holiday season ends, another journey begins, and with it comes the opportunity to refine your budgeting strategies and create a solid plan for the future. It's time to assess this season and make plans for the next. In this chapter, we will explore the importance of planning for next year's gifts, how to set long-term goals for holiday savings, the benefits of starting early, and the invaluable lessons learned from your current budgeting journey.

Reflecting on the Current Year's Budgeting

As the current year draws to a close, it's a perfect time to embark on a journey of reflection. Taking a thoughtful look back at your budgeting efforts can provide invaluable insights that will guide your financial decisions for the upcoming year.

Assessing Achievements and Challenges

Start by assessing your achievements and challenges in the realm of budgeting. Did you meet your savings goals? Were you able to stick to your planned budget throughout the year? Celebrate the milestones you reached, whether it was consistently setting aside funds or finding creative ways to cut costs. Acknowledge the challenges as well, as they provide opportunities for growth and improvement.

Identifying Patterns and Trends

Dig deeper into your budgeting data to identify patterns and trends. Are there certain months when you tend to overspend? Are there specific categories where you consistently give more funds than planned? Understanding these patterns will help you anticipate potential hurdles and make informed adjustments in the future. Perhaps you splurged during holiday sales or underestimated the cost of certain expenses. These insights are stepping stones to more accurate budgeting.

Recognizing Unforeseen Expenses

Life is filled with unexpected surprises, and your budgeting journey is no exception. Take note of any unforeseen expenses that popped up during the year. These could range from medical emergencies to car repairs. While these events can disrupt your financial plans, they also underline the importance of having an emergency fund and being prepared for the unexpected. Continue setting aside funds for your holiday savings, even as you navigate unexpected expenses.

Celebrating Progress and Growth

Reflecting on your budgeting journey is not just about identifying shortcomings; it's also about recognizing your progress and growth. Perhaps you successfully navigated a challenging financial situation or learned to make wiser spending decisions. Celebrate these wins, no matter how small they may seem.

Setting the Stage for a New Beginning

As you reflect on the current year's budgeting efforts, remember that this is a stepping stone to a new beginning. The insights gained from your reflection will lay the foundation for a more informed and strategic approach to budgeting in the upcoming year. Whether you're looking to save more effectively, reduce unnecessary expenses, or better allocate funds to different categories, the knowledge you've acquired is a powerful tool.

Moving Forward with Purpose

Reflection isn't just a one-time exercise; it's a continuous process that informs your financial decisions as you move forward. Use the knowledge you've gained to set clearer goals for the upcoming year. If overspending during the holiday season was a challenge, consider adjusting your savings strategy earlier in the year to accommodate those expenses. If certain categories consistently exceed their budget, explore ways to optimize spending without sacrificing enjoyment.

Setting Long-Term Goals for Holiday Savings

As the joy and festivities of the current holiday season wind down, it's an ideal time to shift your focus toward the future. Setting long-term goals for holiday savings empowers you to approach upcoming seasons with confidence and financial stability.

Defining Your Long-Term Savings Goals

Begin by defining your long-term savings goals for the holiday season. How much do you want to have saved by this time next year? Are there specific trips, gifts, or experiences you're aiming for? Break down this larger goal into smaller, manageable milestones to track your progress along the way.

Establishing a Year-Round Savings Strategy

Long-term holiday savings require a year-round approach. Instead of scrambling to save in the months leading up to the holidays, consider distributing your savings efforts evenly throughout the year. By gradually building up your holiday fund over the course of the year, you're less likely to rely on credit cards or dip into emergency funds to cover expenses. This approach not only reduces the financial burden during the holiday season but also ensures that your budget remains consistent month to month.

Automating Your Long-Term Savings

Automation is a powerful ally in achieving long-term savings goals. If you have not already, set up automatic transfers to your designated holiday savings account on a regular basis. This "set it and forget it" approach ensures that you're consistently contributing to your savings without the need for constant manual intervention. Over time, these contributions accumulate, bringing you closer to your long-term goals.

Navigating Variable Expenses

While setting long-term goals is essential, it's important to acknowledge that holiday expenses can vary from year to year. Unforeseen events, changes in family dynamics, or shifts in financial circumstances can all impact your budget. Embrace the flexibility to adjust your goals and savings strategy as needed to handle these fluctuations.

A Gift to Your Future Self

View your long-term holiday savings efforts as a gift to your future self. The financial security and peace of mind you cultivate today translate into memorable and stress-free celebrations in the years to come. Knowing that you've taken proactive steps to plan for holiday expenses instills a sense of confidence and empowerment.

Starting Early for a Stress-Free Holiday Season

Your daily life is busy, and it's easy to let the holiday season sneak up on you. However, by adopting the practice of starting early, you can gift yourself the invaluable present of a stress-free and enjoyable holiday experience.

Crafting a Well-Structured Timeline

To begin, craft a timeline that outlines the various tasks and goals you want to accomplish leading up to the holiday season. This will include setting up your holiday savings account, creating a preliminary budget, brainstorming gift ideas, and even starting to make or purchase gifts. A well-structured timeline serves as your road map, helping you stay organized and on track.

Early Gift Planning and Purchases

One of the most significant advantages of starting early is the ability to carefully plan and purchase gifts over an extended period. Rather than rushing to buy gifts at the last minute, you can take your time to find thoughtful and meaningful presents that align with your budget. This also opens up opportunities to take advantage of sales, discounts, and promotions throughout the year.

Crafting Homemade Gifts

Starting early provides the ideal opportunity to explore homemade gift options. Whether it's crafting personalized ornaments, baking holiday treats, or creating handmade cards, these DIY gifts require time and care. By beginning your creative projects well in advance, you can invest your energy into crafting meaningful presents that reflect your thoughtfulness.

Enjoying a Relaxed Holiday Season

Perhaps the most significant reward of starting early is the ability to truly savor the holiday season. With your preparations underway, you'll have more time to engage in festive activities, spend quality time with loved ones, and immerse yourself in the joyful spirit of the holidays. This contributes to a more relaxed and fulfilling holiday experience.

Utilizing Lessons Learned for Continuous Improvement

The holiday season is not just a time of joy and celebration; it's also an opportunity for growth and learning. As you conclude the current year's festivities, take a moment to reflect on your experiences and gather insights that can enhance your future holiday celebrations.

Reflecting on Your Accomplishments and Challenges

Before you dive into planning for the next holiday season, set aside time to reflect on the past year's accomplishments and challenges. Consider what worked well in your budgeting and preparations, as well as areas that could use improvement. Were there any unexpected expenses that caught you off guard?

Evaluating Your Gift-Giving Approach

Take a closer look at your gift-giving approach and assess its impact. Did your recipients appreciate and enjoy the gifts you gave? Were there any gifts that felt unnecessary or excessive? Use feedback to refine your gift-giving strategy. Perhaps you discovered that personalized homemade gifts were especially well-received, prompting you to allocate more time for DIY projects next year.

Analyzing Budgeting Strategies

Examine your budgeting strategies and their effectiveness. Did you divide money appropriately to different categories of holiday expenses? Were there any instances where you overspent or could have saved more? By analyzing your budgeting approach, you can fine-tune your allocation of funds, ensuring that you have ample resources for the areas that matter most to you.

Learning from Unexpected Expenses

Unexpected expenses are a reality of life, and they can certainly arise during the holiday season. Review any unexpected costs that you incurred and consider how you can better prepare for them next year. This could involve setting aside a contingency fund or being more vigilant about potential hidden costs, such as travel expenses or last-minute gift needs.

Setting New Goals and Intentions

Armed with the lessons learned from the previous year, set new goals and intentions for the upcoming holiday season. Perhaps you want to issue more budget for experiences and less for material gifts. Or maybe you aim to start your preparations even earlier to reduce stress.

Wrapping It All Up

Reflecting on the current year's budgeting is an investment in your financial future. As you analyze achievements, identify patterns, and acknowledge unforeseen expenses, you're equipping yourself with the wisdom needed to make more informed financial decisions. Set long-term goals for holiday savings to transform your budgeting journey from a short-term endeavor to a lifelong habit. By prioritizing consistent contributions, embracing automation, and adopting a flexible mindset, you're positioning yourself for joyful and stress-free holiday seasons in the future.

Planning for next year's gifts is a journey of foresight and intention. It's about looking beyond the present moment and making conscious decisions that will positively impact your financial well-being. As you enjoy a relaxed and meaningful holiday season, you'll appreciate the wisdom of your decision to start early and the impact it has on both your finances and your overall well-being. By reflecting on your current budgeting efforts, setting long-term goals, starting early, and adapting as needed, you're not only preparing for a stress-free holiday season but also cultivating a healthier relationship with your finances.

Conclusion

We hope that the insights and strategies shared within these pages have illuminated the path to a more intentional, frugal, and joyous holiday season. Budgeting for holiday gifts is not just a financial exercise; it's a way to infuse your celebrations with meaning, minimize stress, and create lasting memories.

Throughout this book, we've explored a wealth of techniques to help you navigate the intricacies of holiday expenses while staying true to your financial goals. From smart shopping strategies and creative gift ideas to the power of the cash envelope method and the magic of automated savings, you've been equipped with a toolkit of actionable approaches.

Remember, the heart of budgeting for holiday gifts lies in aligning your spending with what truly matters to you and your loved ones. By establishing a clear plan, embracing frugal and thoughtful practices, and learning from both successes and challenges, you're well-prepared to create celebrations that reflect your values and aspirations.

As you embark on your journey towards more mindful holiday preparations, we encourage you to apply the strategies that resonate with you. Whether you're utilizing price comparison tools, crafting homemade gifts, engaging with online communities, or exploring part-time gigs, every step you take contributes to a more intentional and enjoyable holiday experience.

Above all, we wish you a holiday season filled with joy, warmth, and meaningful connections. May the gifts you give and receive be a reflection of your love, care, and thoughtfulness. As you celebrate with family and friends, may the memories you create be cherished for years to come.

Thank you for joining us on this journey towards a more thoughtful approach to holiday gifts. Your commitment to intentional celebrations not only benefits your financial well-being but also enriches the lives of those you hold dear. Here's to a successful and joyful holiday season – one that is filled with both cherished moments and wise financial choices.

Wishing you all the best as you embark on your holiday preparations. Happy holidays!